I0606210

★★★★★

MLB TEAMS

Miami MARLINS

KENNY ABDO

abdobooks.com

Published by Abdo Zoom, a division of ABDO, P.O. Box 398166, Minneapolis, Minnesota 55439.

Printed in the United States of America, North Mankato, Minnesota.
102025
012026

Photo Credits: AP Images, Bridgeman Images, Getty Images, Shutterstock
Production Contributors: Kenny Abdo, Jennie Forsberg, Grace Hansen
Design Contributors: Candice Keimig, Neil Klinepier

Library of Congress Control Number: 2025936782

Publisher's Cataloging-in-Publication Data

Names: Abdo, Kenny, author.
Title: Miami Marlins / by Kenny Abdo
Description: Minneapolis, Minnesota : Abdo Zoom, 2026 | Series: MLB teams | Includes online resources and index.
Identifiers: ISBN 9798384940234 (lib. bdg.) | ISBN 9798384940999 (ebook) | ISBN 9798384941378 (read-to-me ebook)
Subjects: LCSH: Miami Marlins (Baseball team)--Juvenile literature. | Baseball teams-Juvenile literature. | Professional sports--Juvenile literature. | Sports franchises-Juvenile literature. | Major League Baseball (Organization)--Juvenile literature.
Classification: DDC 796.357--dc23

Table of CONTENTS

MARLINS

The Miami Marlins have made waves in baseball with two World Series titles, a history full of exciting players, and reeling in big wins!

Miami

From surprising victories to **walk-off** thrills, the Marlins have built a team that keeps the popularity of baseball afloat in Miami.

BATTER UP!

The Marlins joined Major League Baseball (MLB) in 1993 as a member of the **National League** (**NL**). The team was based in Miami and known then as the Florida Marlins. They played their first game against the Dodgers, defeating them 6–3!

The Marlins, in just their fifth year, became the newest team in MLB history to win the World Series. The team was happy when Édgar Rentería walked up to the plate at the bottom of the 11th. The young shortstop hit a line drive up the middle to win it all.

In 2002, the Marlins got new ownership, bringing life to the team. The Marlins shined that season with a strong infield. Second baseman Luis Castillo was a threat at any base. That year, he set a team **record** with a 35-game hitting streak. He also led the majors in stolen bases for the second time with 48.

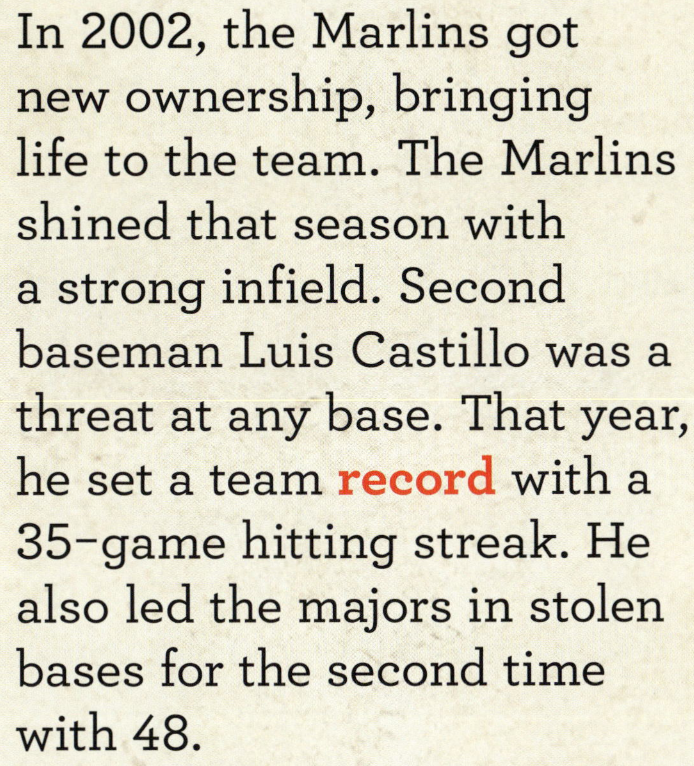

GRAND SLAMS

Things got even better for the Marlins. In 2003, the team took home another World Series win, defeating the Yankees 4–2. **Rookies** such as Dontrelle Willis and Miguel Cabrera made a big impact throughout the series. And Josh Beckett threw a **complete-game shutout** in Game 6 to win it all.

MARLINS

Budweiser
simply

In 2012, the team changed its name to the Miami Marlins. They also got fresh colors and jerseys and a brand new stadium. By the time the Marlins moved into their new ballpark, slugger Giancarlo Stanton had emerged.

HOME
STANTON
27
GOYA
305DEL

Stanton kept playing well for his team. In 2017, he hit 59 homers and won the **NL** MVP Award. He set a team **record** and drove in 132 runs, one of the highest single-season totals in Marlins history.

The Marlins made a surprise playoff appearance in 2020, defeating the Cubs in the opening round of the playoff series. Unfortunately, Miami would fall to the Braves. In 2022, Sandy Alcántara won the **Cy Young Award** after leading the league with six **complete games** and a 2.28 **ERA**.

CY YOUNG AWARD
PRESENTED TO
SANDY ALCANTARA
THE OUTSTANDING
NATIONAL LEAGUE PITCHER
2022

The Marlins reached the playoffs again in 2023. In 2025, the team improved slightly from 2024. Kyle Stowers had a breakout performance and an **All-Star** selection. Xavier Edwards also had a strong season at second base and at bat. With players like that, the Marlins are not far from the top.

CUBS
8 9
R H E
0 0 3 6 0
0 0 1 5 0
EDWARDS
9
Miami
Miami
368

HALL OF FAME

Luis Castillo played for the Marlins from 1996 to 2005. Known for his speed and hitting, he made three **All-Star** teams and won three **Gold Glove Awards**. Castillo had more than 1,200 hits and helped the Marlins win the 2003 World Series. He was named to the Marlins Hall of Fame in 2025.

MARLINS
126
Louisville
Slugger

CABRERA
24

From 2003 to 2007, Miguel Cabrera made a big splash with the Marlins. He was up for **Rookie** of the Year and helped the team win the World Series in 2003. Cabrera hit 138 home runs during his time in Miami. His early success with the Marlins made it no surprise when he went on to become one of the best hitters in baseball.

STANTON
27
Stanton
27

Giancarlo Stanton played for the Marlins from 2010 to 2017 and became one of baseball's biggest stars. He won the **NL** MVP Award in 2017 after hitting 59 home runs, a team **record**. Stanton made four **All-Star** teams while in Miami. He proved to be a big fish in the big leagues!

GLOSSARY

All-Star – consisting of athletes chosen as the best at their positions in a league or region.

complete game – a game in which a starting pitcher stays in the entire game without being relieved.

Cy Young Award – an award given to the best pitcher in the league that season.

Earned-Run Average (ERA) – the average number of earned runs per game scored against a pitcher.

Gold Glove Award – an annual award given to the best fielders at each position in both the American League (AL) and NL.

National League (NL) – one of two 15-team leagues that make up MLB.

record – a top achievement by a player or team that no one has done before.

rookie – a professional athlete in his or her first season on a team.

shutout – a complete game in which a team allows no runs.

walk-off – any victory in which the home team scores the winning run in the bottom of the final inning.

ONLINE RESOURCES

To learn more about the Miami Marlins, please visit **abdobooklinks.com** or scan this QR code. These links are routinely monitored and updated to provide the most current information available.

INDEX